CITIZEN SCIENCE

DATA GEEK

KRISTIN FONTICHIARO

Published in the United States of America by Cherry Lake Publishing
Ann Arbor, Michigan
www.cherrylakepublishing.com

Series Adviser: Kristin Fontichiaro

Photo Credits: Cover and page 1, ©Alohaflaminggo/Shutterstock; page 5, ©Kuzmenko Viktoria photographer/Shutterstock; page 6, ©Christopher Wood/Shutterstock; page 8, ©LuckyImages/Shutterstock; page 10, ©Happy cake Happy café/Shutterstock; page 13, ©Y_L/Shutterstock; page 14, ©Pukhov K/Shutterstock; page 16, ©Vasin Lee/Shutterstock; page 19, ©ESB Basic/Shutterstock; page 20, ©anyaivanova/Shutterstock; page 22, ©Olha Tsiplyar/Shutterstock; page 26, ©iko/Shutterstock; page 28, ©Donna Apsey/Shutterstock

Library of Congress Cataloging-in-Publication Data has been filed and is available at catalog.loc.gov

Cherry Lake Publishing would like to acknowledge the work of the Partnership for 21st Century Learning.
Please visit www.p21.org for more information.

Printed in the United States of America
Corporate Graphics

ABOUT THE AUTHOR

Kristin Fontichiaro teaches and studies how people learn about and use data at the University of Michigan School of Information.

TABLE OF CONTENTS

CHAPTER 1

Why Citizen Science Is Needed

The world is always changing. So are the plants, animals, weather, water, and land of our planet. Figuring out why things change is important for lots of people, from farmers and sailors to professors and researchers.

Imagine these three problems in nature:

Problem 1: A scientist at a local university wants to know on what date crocus flowers bloom all over North America. Many people say that when crocuses bloom, it's a sign that spring has really arrived. The scientist would like to know if this is true or just a saying. She and her small team could drive around every town in the United States looking for crocuses. This would take years. Because the crocus season is so short, she could only collect

While it might be fun to drive across the country looking for crocuses in bloom, it would also be extremely expensive and time-consuming.

a little **data**, or information, each year. It would also require a lot of money. It costs a lot to travel across the country! Maybe after a career of looking, she would have a better sense of when and where crocuses bloom. Isn't there a way to get data about crocus blooms faster and at lower cost?

Problem 2: Bees are really important for **agriculture**. They carry pollen from flower to flower. This allows the plants to reproduce. But the bee population has been way down for the past few years. A farmer wants to know if planting more

It's not easy to collect data about animals that live in remote areas, such as polar bears.

honeysuckle (a favorite plant of bees) will raise the number of bees. So he plants more honeysuckle, but later he still counts fewer bees at his hive. Was something wrong with his land? The honeysuckle? Something else? He doesn't know, but he's worried.

Problem 3: As our **climate** changes and the planet grows warmer, polar bears are among the animal species being threatened. A zoologist would like to know if these bears are changing their grooming habits as the temperature creeps upward. She could camp out in the polar ice caps, where the bears live, and observe them day after day. However, then she would have to miss teaching at her university. How can she learn about polar bear habits and still keep teaching?

In each of these situations, problems could be solved faster if time, money, or **scale** weren't an issue. What if there was a way to get more people involved so the work could be done more rapidly? What if those people were volunteers? Each person would give a small amount of their time because they think that doing a little bit of science work is fun. That's what happens with **citizen science** projects.

Citizen science relies on ordinary, interested citizen volunteers to help speed along scientific understanding. Usually, citizen

Once data has been collected by volunteers, researchers can begin studying it to see what they can learn.

science projects are about **biology**, or the study of plants and animals. But some citizen science projects can involve water, weather, or land.

Most of the time, citizen science projects are led by an expert (like the farmer) or researcher (like the zoologist or the crocus researcher) who designs an experiment and then educates volunteers to help gather data correctly. The volunteers collect the data. Then the experts **analyze** and make sense of it. Some projects may take only a few days and then end. Still other projects may be repeated year after year to see how things change over time.

Experts benefit from citizen science experiments because they gain a lot of help in doing their research. Good research requires a lot of data. When volunteers get involved, the experts can collect one or more of the following:

- *more* data
- data from a *wider variety* of sources (from more farms or more states)
- data that *costs less* to collect
- data that *takes less time* to collect

To do research, most experts have to raise money from organizations, government agencies, or individual donors. So citizen science has a lot of appeal!

Volunteers enjoy participating in citizen science projects for a lot of different reasons. Some enjoy learning more about how scientists work. Some teachers and students enjoy getting out of the classroom and being part of the nature that they normally study in textbooks. Sometimes, entire families enjoy doing data collection together. And some volunteers are drawn to citizen science projects because they care about their communities and want to help make the world around them healthier and safer.

One way you might participate in citizen science is by taking photos of wildlife or plants.

In this book, you'll learn more about citizen science practices. You'll also discover some ways that you, your family, or even your school can be involved in contributing to the professional scientific community. We'll even share a few projects that have the same volunteer-based, **crowdsourced** spirit as citizen science, but without the science. Let's get started!

Crowdsourcing

Citizen science is a form of crowdsourcing, in which large numbers of people work together to achieve large goals. Wikipedia is probably the most famous example of a crowdsourced project. Its entries are authored by literally thousands of different volunteer authors and editors. Some people say the Internet itself is crowdsourced. This is because its pages are made up of content from millions of people, organizations, businesses, and governments.

CHAPTER 2

What Do Citizen Science Projects Look Like?

What might citizen science projects look like in the real world? Let's think back to the three problems we talked about in chapter one.

Problem 1: Imagine the crocus researcher creates a site online. The site includes training information and advice on how to spot a crocus. It includes photos of all colors of crocuses and the various stages of bloom so visitors will know exactly what the researcher means by "in bloom." She invites volunteers from all over the country to log in and record their locations and the dates on which they first saw crocuses. These volunteers upload photos so the researcher can quickly check if they are identifying the flowers correctly. After all, the information would not be useful if people were mistaking crocuses for daffodils.

As crocus flowers bloom, their petals gradually open wider and wider. A good citizen science project needs to tell volunteers which stage counts as "in bloom" to have accurate data collection.

The sweet nectar in honeysuckle plants is a source of food for bees. In our example, the farmer recruits other farmers to test his theory that more honeysuckle will attract more bees.

Within a few weeks, the researcher has enough data on crocus blooms to complete her project and share her findings with the scientific community. Now her fellow scientists have more insight and ideas to apply to their own investigations. In addition, the people who grow, package, and sell crocus bulbs have information they can use to improve their business and make more money. Meanwhile, our researcher can move on to learn about a different aspect of nature. Over the course of her career, she will have time to make many more discoveries than she would have without the help of volunteers.

Problem 2: The farmer goes to his local farm **cooperative** and explains his **hypothesis** about honeysuckle attracting more bees and increasing the bee population. He convinces 50 other farmers to participate. Half will add honeysuckle near their beehives next season. The other half will not. The farmers agree on a common technique for counting their bees. They also agree to count them on the first day of each month. Each person gets a worksheet to

Why Does Planning Matter?

In this chapter, you read a lot about the importance of having a plan for research. Why is planning so important? Think of it this way: Have you ever gone to the grocery store without a list? You probably came home with a few extra things you didn't plan to buy. You might also have forgotten one or two things you needed. A list would have helped you save money and get everything you needed, right?

Research works the same way. An expert needs to make sure that everyone on the team knows just what to do. After all, that person probably will not be there when the others are collecting data. If the volunteers are supposed to measure rainfall in centimeters, but they don't know that, the researcher could end up with data measured in inches. Imagine what a mess that would be! Good researchers know that detailed planning leads to an effective use of volunteers.

Think about the environment around you. What would you like to learn and communicate to decision makers? Good citizen science projects can influence government laws and funding.

fill in with a pencil. The farmer leading the study gives the other participants a cutting from his honeysuckle plant. This means the experiment won't cost anyone anything to start. It also ensures that everyone has the same kind of honeysuckle.

Now the farmer will be able to compare data and better understand whether honeysuckle has an effect on the local bee population.

Problem 3: The zoologist makes one trip to the polar ice caps and sets up a camera that automatically takes photos every five seconds. Those photos are sent via satellite to her lab in New

Mexico. They are then uploaded to a Web site where volunteers add descriptive code words to each photo. After four weeks, the zoologist has enough data to have a better understanding of what polar bears are doing. She accomplishes this all while staying nice and warm in the Southwest.

In each of the examples above, working together makes it possible to learn more than any one person could do alone. That's the power of citizen science.

For a citizen science project to be accurate and successful, there are some important elements that need to be present:

- *Someone who is in charge of and organizes the project.* Most of the time, this is a researcher or professor. However, citizen science projects can also be organized by science museums, conservation groups, or concerned individuals. The person in charge is often called the principal investigator or lead researcher. This person is tasked with designing the experiment and answering questions like: "What are we studying?" "What data are we collecting and for what purpose?" "When and how will we collect data?" "What is the common vocabulary we will use to describe the **phenomena** we see or measure?" "How will we sort, analyze, and make sense of the data?"

- *A clear discussion of the problem.* What will the team try to figure out by collecting data? Asking this question will make sure everybody understands the purpose of the project and why it is important. It will also help the experts recruit volunteers. People want to know that their efforts are going toward something that is important to them.

- *A way to recruit volunteers.* Some scientists use Web sites such as SciStarter.com or Zooniverse.org, which coordinate many citizen science projects at once. The idea of these sites is to make it easy for people to find projects and to stay connected with citizen science when their current project concludes. Local citizen science projects might also use newspaper notices, flyers, presentations at city council or environmental club meetings, or social media to recruit volunteers.

- *Trained volunteers.* In the crocus-counting example, it's important that volunteers know what a crocus looks like and what it means to be "in bloom." With the bees, the farmer holds a discussion with his neighbors about a method for counting bees and gives them each a checklist so they will collect data the same way.

If a researcher carefully explains the details of a project to her volunteer data collectors, she is more likely to end up with high-quality data.

- *A way of checking that the data is accurate.* The crocus researcher does this by asking people to send photos of their crocuses so she can check that they're counting the right kind of flowers. The farmer does this by giving everybody the same worksheet to fill in. He also explains how to count the bees and on which date. The zoologist's computer randomly shows her one in every 20 photos so she can check a researcher's accuracy without having to review every photo.

Preparing a report is one way for a researcher to share the results of a study with colleagues and other people who might be interested.

- *A plan for analyzing the data.* This is usually the expert's job. Whether this person counts results by hand or sets up a complex computer program to sort the data into patterns, someone has to make sense of everything that has been collected.

- *A plan for sharing what has been learned and taking action.* Reports, presentations, posters, and meetings are all ways the team can share what they have learned with others.

CHAPTER 3

Finding Citizen Science Projects

So, you've decided to become involved in researching the natural world? Great! But how can you get started?

First, think about whether you want to do a project alone or with members of your class, family, or community. Working by yourself is often convenient. But think about the benefits of working with others. You can carpool together if you are doing work in a specific location. Fellow volunteers can also help you stay motivated. Ask your family members, classmates, or people at your library if they would like to participate with you. You might be surprised to discover that other citizen scientists are already right around you!

For some people, heading outside to collect data about nature is a lot of fun!
However, others would rather find ways to help while staying at home.

Paying to Volunteer?

It isn't common, but some citizen science projects charge their volunteers a small fee. That might seem unfair at first. You might ask yourself, "Why would I pay to do volunteer work?"

However, things aren't always that simple. In some cases, volunteering for citizen science requires being bused to a particular location, being trained, receiving special equipment, or even getting insurance to cover you in case you get hurt while volunteering. These costs would add up quickly if the researchers had to pay for everyone who participated. Paying a small fee makes it possible for the research to be conducted.

Next, think about whether you would like to participate in an online project or one where you collect field data in real life. Some people love being out in the fresh air and collecting data in the wild. Others may have allergies, transportation difficulty, or no projects in their area. Or they might have trouble getting around. And some people may prefer just working online. Don't be afraid to consider these people, as well. Keep in mind that some projects ask you to collect data in nature and then report results online.

You'll also want to think about what kind of research topics interest you most. There are citizen science projects to study insects, birds, mammals, water, astronomy, climate, and more. You might consider calling your local nature center or science museum to see if there are local projects going on. Or you could go online and do a search for the topic you are interested in and your state. Remember that when you search online, you can skip capital letters when you are typing! For example, a good search might be: *"citizen science" butterflies michigan.* We put citizen science in quotation marks so that the search engine will only show results in which those two words are right next to each other. That will help you get better results back.

Still looking for projects? In the next chapter, we'll look at some well-known citizen science projects online that you might enjoy.

Projects to Join

Here are some well-known citizen science projects you might enjoy exploring.

Zooniverse

www.zooniverse.org

This site features many projects from universities looking for help with research on the arts, climate, animals, flowers, medicine, nature, space, and more. You will need to create an account, so ask an adult for permission before you get started. On a cold, rainy night, you might stay warm and dry at home while helping the Cleveland Metroparks identify wild animals in photos taken by remote cameras and posted to Zooniverse. You would watch a tutorial to learn how to use the site and even see a deer with

One of the great things about citizen science is that many helpful projects can be done from the comfort of your own home.

antlers! You might also help look for ridges on the surface of Mars. You can complete several identification tasks during a TV commercial break. Try it!

SciStarter

https://scistarter.com

Like Zooniverse, SciStarter is an online platform that hosts many citizen science projects, as well as a few you can complete offline. Examples include projects to help NASA identify clouds, track the flu in your community, and monitor air quality. SciStarter has fewer active projects than Zooniverse, so check both before you get started.

Foldit

http://fold.it

You probably already know that your body is made of billions and billions of cells. But did you know that inside those cells are some real superstar workers called proteins? These proteins do a lot of heavy lifting to help your body process food and power your muscles. Proteins are made out of long strings of connected molecules called amino acids. However, amino acids don't like to line up in straight lines. Instead, long-chained proteins fold up into different shapes. The kind of shape the protein makes tells

Do you get a lot of birds in your backyard? You might have a lot of valuable information to offer researchers!

scientists what it does. Researchers want to know how they can make better drugs, and knowing the shapes proteins are folded into is part of the key to doing this.

At Fold.it, you can play a game that helps researchers at the University of Washington gain insights into proteins. Hopefully, this will one day help lead to cures for diseases such as HIV/AIDS, cancer, and Alzheimer's disease.

[21ST CENTURY SKILLS LIBRARY]

Feeder Watch

http://feederwatch.org

Do you keep a bird feeder in your yard or on a balcony or stoop? Or maybe you have a birdbath or plants that attract birds? If so, you might be able to help Cornell University's famous Lab of **Ornithology**! With the help of an adult, you can register to count your feathered visitors, log in online, and share your observations from November through early April. There is a small fee for participation, but in exchange, you receive training materials, a bird poster, and a magazine. You'll also get the final report so you can see how your contributions paid off when combined with other U.S. and Canadian bird-watchers!

Journey North

www.learner.org/jnorth/

Journey North asks you to participate in citizen science activities that help track seasonal changes. Whether looking at plant blooms, animal **migration**, or changes in the sun's position, humans have many ways to provide important data that helps monitor the change in seasons.

Contributing to citizen science isn't just good for research. It's also a way to learn more about the world we live in. It's a win-win. Have fun, citizen scientists!

Citizen Science Without the Science: Crowdsourcing Projects

Do you like the idea of crowdsourcing, but you aren't a fan of science? Here are some projects to explore:

- *Zooniverse.org isn't just science! Find projects about the arts and history here, too. You can study everything from Shakespeare to war diaries.*
- *Smithsonian Digital Volunteers (http://transcription.si.edu) has a wealth of photographs of written text. You can help by reading the text in the photograph and typing in what you see. The digital text can then be searched by future researchers. Explore letters, photo albums, diaries, and more.*
- *Wikipedia is the world's most famous crowdsourced Web site. You can contribute what you know about the world to this enormous online encyclopedia. But watch out! If you make a mistake, your information could be deleted or fixed by someone else!*

For More Information

BOOKS

Fontichiaro, Kristin. *Big Data*. Ann Arbor, MI: Cherry Lake Publishing, 2018.

Oehrli, Jo Angela. *Ethical Data Use*. Ann Arbor, MI: Cherry Lake Publishing, 2018.

WEB SITES

FeederWatch
http://feederwatch.org
Contribute to citizen science by sharing your observations of birds.

Zooniverse
www.zooniverse.org
Contribute to a wide variety of crowdsourcing and citizen science projects! Ask an adult before you set up an account.

GLOSSARY

agriculture (AG-ri-kuhl-chur) farming of crops and animals

analyze (AN-uh-lize) to study information or data, sometimes using math, to try to find patterns or meaning

biology (by-AH-luh-jee) the study of life and all living things

citizen science (SIT-ti-zuhn SYE-uhns) ordinary people working to help experts gather data about science

climate (KLYE-mit) the weather typical of a place over a long period of time

cooperative (koh-AH-pur-uh-tiv) a business owned by all the people who work in it and who share the responsibilities and the profits

crowdsourced (CROWD-sorsd) relying on help from many people who each contribute a small part to a project

data (DAY-tuh) information, often in number form

hypothesis (hye-PAH-thi-sis) an idea that could explain how something works but still has to be tested to be proven correct

migration (mye-GRAY-shun) the movement of animals from one location to another at certain times of the year

ornithology (or-nih-THAH-luh-jee) the scientific study of birds

phenomena (fuh-NAH-muh-nah) scientific events

scale (SKALE) the size of something compared to something else

INDEX